A M A Z I N G
LOOK-ALIKES™

JOAN STEINER

Photography by Thomas Lindley

WALKER BOOKS
AND SUBSIDIARIES
LONDON · BOSTON · SYDNEY

The author wishes to express heartfelt thanks to Thomas Lindley for his superb photographic work, and to Megan Shaw Tingley, her editor, and Amy Berkower, her agent, for the unflagging support and enthusiasm they have shown for Look-Alikes from the very beginning. Thanks also go to Paul Richer of *Sesame Street* magazine, who originally commissioned several of these images.

First published 1999 by Little, Brown and Company, USA

First published in Great Britain 2001 by Walker Books Ltd
87 Vauxhall Walk, London SE11 5HJ

This edition published 2002

2 4 6 8 10 9 7 5 3 1

© 1999, 2002 Joan Steiner
Photography by Thomas Lindley

The Bedroom scene was photographed by Jeff Heiges

This book has been typeset in Futura and ATGoudy

Printed in Hong Kong

British Library Cataloguing in Publication Data:
a catalogue record for this book
is available from the British Library

ISBN 0-7445-8952-5

Come visit a land of wild surprises
Where common objects wear disguises!
Peanuts can look like a teddy bear,
Kiwi fruit like the pad for a chair.
At least fifty look-alikes in each scene
 (but two).
Find some or all – it's up to you.
The sweetie clock will count the hours
As you test your detective powers…
And if you're really keeping track,
You'll find your answers at the back!

Happy Hunting!

To Look-Alike Land! We're blasting full throttle
On a spaceship that looks like a THERMOS BOTTLE.

Let's start our visit at this house.
That rock on the lawn looks like a TOY MOUSE!

Here is the kitchen, so come on in.
The sink looks like a SARDINE TIN.

This is the sitting-room, if you couldn't tell.
That lampshade looks like a little brass BELL.

Here's the bedroom and the bathroom as well.
The sink in the bathroom looks like a SHELL.

Here's the school bus, right on time.
Each rear-view mirror looks like a DIME.

This classroom has books and paints and blocks.
The teacher's desk looks like a TISSUE BOX.

It's movie time – c'mon, boys and girls!
See those lights 'round the poster? They look just like PEARLS.

The building site is straight ahead
With paving stones that look like BREAD.

Here at the farm you can feed the geese
By the puddle that looks like a JIGSAW PIECE.

We hope that you will come back soon!
The signal-post looks like a WOODEN SPOON.
It's signalling, *"Bye, bye – for now!"*

EXTRA CHALLENGE

I don't always look the same
But I'm always long and lean.
Can you tell me: What's my name?
I'm found in every scene.

Hint: Keep a sharp lookout!

PLAY THE LOOK-ALIKES GAME

Search for look-alikes with a friend.
Take turns at finding *one*.
And when one of you is at wit's end,
That's when the game is done.

HOW TO COUNT THE LOOK-ALIKES

1. If more than one of the same object is used to make up *one* look-alike (such as ten pencils making up a fence), it counts as *one* look-alike. But if the same or a similar object appears elsewhere in the scene to make a *different* look-alike (such as a pencil appearing as a flagpole), it counts again.

2. Miniatures don't count as look-alikes unless they appear as something different from a larger version of themselves. For example, a toy car that represents a real car is not a look-alike. But a toy car that looks like a fire hydrant *does* count.

3. As long as you can identify an object, you don't have to get the name exactly right.

THE LOOK-ALIKES

*Asterisks indicate hard-to-find items –
for super sleuths only!*

ROCKET SHIP
- *53 Look-Alikes*

IN THE SKY: Rhinestones, star-shaped button, rhinestone ring, pearl, foil and plastic stars, yellow and orange M&M sweets, marble, acorn, round button, popper, pearl earring, jingle bell, starfish, blue faceted bead, tiny seashell, Christmas bauble.
ROCKET SHIP: **Left to right:** Wheat, batteries, spool of thread, birthday candle, Thermos bottle, rubber spatula, nappy pin, sticks of chewing-gum, sheet of loose-leaf paper, sweetcorn kernel, red and green M&M sweets, dime, pasta spirals, pencil-tip rubber, two-tone rubber, Lego piece, white pencil, marker pen, paintbrush, card of buttons, red paper-clip, price tag, postage stamp, magnetic letter "T", nail clipper, metal buckle, shuttlecock. ASTRONAUT: Opera glasses, Ping-Pong ball, ponytail elastic, macaroni, striped seashell, screw, yellow button, tea bag, tubes of paint, clumps of cotton wool.

HOUSE
- *54 Look-Alikes*

TREES: **Left to right:** Rope, baguette, leather glove, dog figurine, green paper doilies, antler. GARAGE AND DRIVEWAY ITEMS: TV antenna, plastic hanger, paper matches, protractor, champagne cork muzzle, blackboard. **Car:** Red shoe, peace symbol, buttons, hair-grip. **Lawnmower:** Sunglasses, padlock. LAWN, GARDEN AND PATH: Towel, doggie treat, panpipe, chess piece (bishop), tap aerator, pencil sharpener, wooden ballpoint pen, bunch of (artificial) grapes, embroidery hoop, catnip mouse, arrow, pencils, jigsaw puzzle pieces, poppy seeds*, mints (tricycle wheels). HOUSE: Maize, brick, matzoh, pretzel twists, tea bags, peanuts, dog biscuits, book, seashell, accordion expanding wall hooks, venetian mini-blind, comb, wooden forks, baby bottle teat, birthday candles, gum rubbers, coin purse, crayons, wallet, paper fastener, whistle.

KITCHEN

• *94 Look-Alikes*

ABOVE CUPBOARDS: Spools of thread, cherry tomato, postage stamp, small bar of soap, sea-urchin shell, gold foil sweet wrapper. CUPBOARDS, WINDOW AND DOOR: Wallet, dollar bill, white dominoes, colour sampler, vacuum-cleaner attachment, toggle buttons, crayon, cotton buds, broccoli, cards of buttons, rulers, M&M sweets (doorknobs). COUNTER AREA: **Left of stove:** Birthday candles, chewing-gum pieces, paper-clip dispenser (with paper-clips), tiny white buttons, night-light, fuse, crayon tips, magnifying glass, adaptor, envelope, powder puffs, bars of soap. **Stove:** Museum admission tag, tiny chess pieces, stick of chewing-gum (wrapped), tiny ravioli, harmonica, toy spiders, red Christmas bauble, Walkman, poppers, thermometers. **Right of stove:** Nappy pin, eyeshadow applicator, spool of blue thread, acorn, biscuit, door-latch hook, sardine tin, stock cube, vegetable peeler, Gummy Bears sweet, hair-grip, pencil sharpener, bottle caps, sink plug, photographic slide, floppy disk, tiny black buttons*. STEP STOOL AND FLOOR: Staplers, dominoes, pages of calendar, white chocolate bar, pan scourer. REFRIGERATOR AND CLOSET AREA: Mint sweet, big white button, pencil-tip rubber, peanut, seven-day pill-box, postage stamp, crochet hooks, eyeshadow box, salt shaker, fake fingernail, small pencils, triple wall hook, toy teacups, individual coffee creamer, ice cube tray, dental mirror, paintbrush, green thimble, bubble-gum (unwrapped), razor, tube of paint. TABLE AREA: Tap aerator (ceiling light), Cheese Puffs, breadsticks, dog-biscuits, embroidery hoop with fabric, silver thimble, jellybeans, Ritz cracker, paper-fastener, wooden clothes-pegs, place mat.

SITTING-ROOM

• *70 Look-Alikes*

ALONG THE WALLS: **Left to right:** Maple seeds, seed packet, green ribbon, compact disc, brass drawer handle, kernels of sweetcorn, crayons, candied fruit slices, lasagne strips, tiny white buttons, doorstops, tiny gold safety-pins, leaves (real and artificial), gold buckle, gold bracelet, postage stamp. FURNITURE, LEFT-HAND SIDE: **Television:** Eyeshadow box, ball-headed pin. **Cabinet:** Wrapped chocolate bar, crackers. **Reading lamp:** Bell, ball-peen hammer, paperweight. **Armchair:** Peapod, candle, chess pieces (knights and bishops). **Dining area:** Christmas biscuits, tambourine, spool of thread. **Rocking-chair:** Hair-grips, hairpins, slice of kiwi fruit. **Planter:** Napkin ring. FIREPLACE: Old Christmas bauble, peppermint sweet, grummet*, toy diamond ring, marble, doll's shoes, silk autumn leaf, magnets, cinnamon sticks, chocolate bar, paper binder clip. FURNITURE, RIGHT-HAND SIDE: **Grandfather clock:** Chess piece (pawn), toy compass, egg timer/hourglass. **Pink chair:** Two pincushions, doggie treat, pen nibs. **Sofa:** Toiletries/make-up bag, fruit-filled biscuit, ravioli, angel-wing biscuits. **Coffee table:** Roll of ribbon, bottle cap. **Easy chair:** Oven glove. **Metal table:** Large compass, hose nozzle. **Side table:** Pencil, sea-urchin shell, leather wallet insert, Pirouline tubular biscuits, comb. ON THE FLOOR: Clothing label, place mat, spinach burrito wrapper, more postage stamps, fig roll biscuit, slice of salami.

BEDROOM

• *67 Look-Alikes*

CEILING AND WALLS: Paper plate, (part of) bubble-blowing wand, sink plug, Ping-Pong ball, paper doll's clothes, fruit biscuits, tortilla chips, T-shirt, animal crackers, socks, cotton buds, broccoli, pink hair-grip. BATHROOM: Postage stamps, dice, Wheat Thins crackers, paper umbrella, dummy, seashell, tube of paint, jingle bells, tiny key. BEDROOM FURNISHINGS: **Bed:** Red crayons, peanuts (teddy bear), alphabet blocks, pasta spirals, bread roll, red comb. **Bookcase:** Pencils, sticks of chewing-gum, rubber ball, Lego pieces, Gummy Bears sweet*. **Bureau:** Cap of toothpaste tube, spool of thread, green buttons, orange and white plastic harmonica, orange toothbrush. **Toy basket:** Ball of twine, plastic toothpick, toy flagpole stick, candle, red party streamer, chess piece (knight), crayon. **Laundry basket:** Calculator. **Desk and chair:** Pretzel twist, pretzel sticks, Ritz cracker, seashell, unshelled almond, dollar bill, yellow party streamer roll, sticks of green clay. ON THE FLOOR: Custard creams, doll's shoe, poppers, birthday candle, spiral seashell, gum rubber, cherry tomato, Life Saver sweets, screw, dog biscuits, roll caps (for cap gun), tangerine, pot holder.

SCHOOL BUS

• *48 Look-Alikes*

ACROSS THE STREET: Pretzel sticks, spiral notepads, Life Saver sweet, luggage tag, skirt fastener, Scrabble tiles, belt buckle, pink rubber, sponge penguin bath toy, pretzel twists, crackers, cinnamon sticks, spool of thread, nuts (nuts-and-bolts type), tiny popper. BUS: Windscreen ice scraper, hose sprinkler attachment, hair-grip, ruler, magnetic pick-up stick, birthday candles, tent stakes, pencils, tiny plastic clothes-pegs, sports radio, pencil-tip rubber, buttons, felt-tip pen, M&M sweets, chocolate-covered doughnuts, jacks, domino, crayons, nappy pins, drawing-pin, nail clippers, dimes, pushpin, chess piece (bishop), wristwatch face. FOREGROUND: Broccoli, red pistachio nuts, green feathers, flannels, popcorn, breadsticks, small slices of bread, peapods.

CLASSROOM

- *67 Look-Alikes*

CEILING: Loose-leaf binder with paper, marshmallows. ALONG WALLS: **Left-hand wall:** Spiral seashell, acorn cap, metal-edged ruler, dollar bill, balloons, blue comb, dog biscuits, starfish, lettuce, bull-dog paper-clip, paintbrush. **Back wall:** Yardstick, alphabet blocks, small box of tissues, red pencil sharpener, die, pencil-tip rubber, package-carrying handle, soap dish, raisin boxes, card of drawing-pins, paint-box with brush, jellybean, scallop seashell, wrist-watch face, caramels, toy train freight cars, pencils (two kinds for easel), wishbone, playing-card, two green books (blackboard), sink plug, bird's egg, clear plastic coin purse, Goldfish crackers, brown rice*, paddleball toy, sticks of blue clay, feathers, spool of crochet thread. **Right-hand wall:** Paintbrush (flagpole), lollipop, button. IN CENTRE OF ROOM: Spiral notepads, crayons, cut-off pencils, cream crackers, price tag, slate chalkboard, wooden clothes-pegs, white beads (square and round), wooden match, postage stamps (drawings), hook (hook-and-eye type), pineapple ring, white jar lid*, sticks of chalk, birthday candle, silver thimble, afro comb, large box of tissues, chess pieces (pawns), scissors, another postage stamp (book), serpentine party streamer.

CINEMA LOBBY

- *54 Look-Alikes*

CEILING: Hubcap, jingle bell, gold buttons, jacks. HANGING LAMPS: Glass doorknob, wooden ballpoint pen with cap, doorbell, candle. LOBBY WALLS, ENTRANCE-WAY AND TICKET WINDOW: Red golf tees, red pick-up sticks, red pencils, bulldog paper-clips, string of pearls, red comb, playing-cards, shelf brackets, coins (dimes and 100-peso pieces), silver ballpoint pens, dental scrapers, spanner, table knives, toy compass, toothbrush and mug holder, cinema tickets. LOBBY FLOOR AND FREE-STANDING ITEMS: Pennies, gold hoop earring, meat thermometer, wooden ruler, jigsaw puzzle pieces, doorstops, paper-clip dispenser (with paper-clip), brass hose nozzle, tiny safety-pin, protractor. REFRESHMENT STAND AREA: Paper fan, toothbrushes, plastic coin purse, pencil sharpener with shavings holder, alphabetti spaghetti*, starfish, silver pencil sharpener, plastic thimble, cut-off crayons, digital watch, Lucite salt shaker/pepper mill, stock cubes, dice, address book with pencil, dollar bill, price tag, tiny watercolour paint-box, harmonica, leather wallet, dental floss dispenser.

BUILDING SITE

• *94 Look-Alikes*

BEYOND THE FENCE: **Left to right:** Bricks, ink bottle, shoe polish tin, merchandise stamps, dog biscuits, broccoli, lipstick, bingo cards, admission tickets*, address book, ice-cream cone, wafer biscuits, dice, lantern, silverware storage tray, sardine tin, ballpoint pen and holder, restaurant order pad. AEROPLANE: Tube of paint, guitar pick, tiny nut (nuts-and-bolts type)*, transparent button*. FENCE: Pretzel sticks. IN THE PIT: **Construction shed:** Spiral notepad, UPC label. **Yellow crane:** Walkman-style radio, staple remover, pencil, disposable-blade knives, hexagonal breakfast cereal, black buttons, squishy fishing lure. **Blue steamroller:** Candles, nail-clipper, screw, magnetic letters and numbers (F, Z, 1, 7). **Black building frame:** CD storage rack, CD jewel cases. **Red excavator:** Camera, penknife, key-holder, wind-up mechanical teeth, pushpin, gold bracelet, red foil stars. **Small yellow crane:** Toy giraffe, wooden matches. **Blue tower crane:** T-square/metal ruler, clear plastic ruler, box of matches, nappy pin, weighted fish-hook. **White building frame:** Carpenter's folding rules (opened), wire shower caddies, matzoh, small bar of soap*, sticks of chewing-gum. **Orange trailer:** Spirit-level, orange Life Saver sweets. **Cement mixer:** Mustard bottle, postage stamp, padlock, (part of a) flexible drinking straw, metal whistle with orange cord, small pencil, plastic whistle, staplers, shoehorn, birthday candle, rolls of black electrician's tape, jacks, spool of green thread. **Individual items at the site, left to right:** Desk lamp, brownies with nuts, carpenter's folding rule (folded), shelled walnuts, coffee beans, gum rubbers, ballpoint pen, cotton buds, felt-tip pen, embroidery hoop. FOREGROUND: Bird seed, crayons, dog biscuits, small slices of bread, tweezers, big black button, (Note: tiny bucket is a miniature rather than a look-alike), cinnamon sticks, peppermint stick, red M&M sweet, clamps, breadsticks, jeans label.

FARM SCENE

• *70 Look-Alikes*

TO LEFT OF ROAD: **From top:** Tartan zip-up bag*, cushions, green pan scourer, green gumdrops, leaf-shaped mint sweets, sock, flannel, metal hinge, (Note: toy truck is a miniature rather than a look-alike), dime wrapper with dime, lipstick, bunch of (artificial) grapes, doormat, peanut (in trailer)*, wagon-wheel pasta, potato croquettes, (part of) stuffed animal, potatoes (red and white), parsley (in many places), pot holder, angel-wing biscuit, green beans (several places), peacock feathers, corduroy trousers. **Tractor:** Red hair-grip, parcel tape dispenser, black popper (steering wheel)*, inflator needle, paper-clip, big button, assorted nuts (hazelnuts and Brazil nuts), burnt matchsticks, green jellybeans (in several places), green hair ties ("scrunchies"). ROAD: Tan tie, hamster food. TO RIGHT OF ROAD: Gold pan scourer, pastry cutter, green dog biscuits, pot-holder loom with green loops, dark green velvety glove, toy fawn, batteries (AA and AAA), chequered place mat. BARN: Toolbox, earring, green padlock, cake decorator nozzle, thimble, ladle, plastic drinking straw, key, aerosol can, toy train track, dominoes, candied fruit slice, cotton buds, croutons. FARMYARD: Cinnamon sticks, fur (two kinds), brown crayon, old-fashioned roller-skate, pencils (two kinds), ball of twine, coffee tin, copper funnel, garlic cloves, jigsaw puzzle piece, peanut, Brazil nut, coffee beans.

CHOO-CHOO TRAIN

• *46 Look-Alikes*

SMOKE: Clumps of cotton wool. TRAIN: **Locomotive:** Sink aerator, jar of model paint, tiny brass bracket, roll of film, lamp socket, yellow Life Saver sweet*, torch, spiral notepad, toy school bus, pennies, spool of black thread, big black buttons, tiny paper binder clip, can-opener, spanner, (artificial) daisies. **Tender:** Tea tin with tea, sewing-machine bobbins (on next two cars as well). **Passenger car:** Watercolour paint-box, pencils, birthday candles, melba toast, afro comb, package-carrying handle, dog biscuits, dollar bill, corn-on-the-cob holder. **Freight car:** Ruler, batteries, fishing float, tiny key, more pennies, wallet, dollar bills, clothing label. LANDSCAPE: Green blanket, tweed jacket, woollen hat, parsley, jigsaw pieces. SIGNAL POST: Wooden spoon, top of a Thermos, red and green Life Saver sweets. TRACKS: Brown electrical flex, sticks of chewing-gum (unwrapped).

ANSWER TO EXTRA CHALLENGE: *Pencil.*

JOAN STEINER is a graduate of Barnard College in New York City, and the recipient of numerous art and design awards, including a Society of Illustrators Award and a National Endowment for the Arts fellowship. Her first book, *Super Look-Alikes*, received glowing reviews and was featured on national television in the USA. Joan Steiner lives in Claverack, New York.